Giving up the Game: How to Win in Real Estate

Emmitt Hayes

Published by EH3 DISTRIBUTION, 2022.

While every precaution has been taken in the preparation of this book, the publisher assumes no responsibility for errors or omissions, or for damages resulting from the use of the information contained herein.

GIVING UP THE GAME: HOW TO WIN IN REAL ESTATE

First edition. April 11, 2022.

ISBN: 979-8201036294

Written by Emmitt Hayes.

Also by Emmitt Hayes

Giving up the Game: How to Win in Real Estate

Table of Contents

This book is dedicated to all the people who never gave up when things didn't go right for them the first time. Life is a marathon and as long as you keep pushing you will always win in the long run. Slow and steady wins the race.

Chapter 1 (Intro)

J ulius Caesar said that 'experience is the best teacher'. When you are knowledgeable about a particular job, task, or field of study, you become the one who is experienced. With the knowledge you gain, things are simpler, and you become more efficient and productive. You do not waste time, effort, money, or assets once you gain experience and knowledge. Hayes Realty has over 16 years in the real estate game as agents, brokers, and real estate investors, in one of the hottest markets in America, Los Angeles.

You better believe we have major experience and have dealt with the ups and downs in this real estate game. We give the people the game, the straight-up know-how, on what to do and what not to do in real estate. We have made many mistakes trying to figure out the real estate game, so now others can benefit from those mistakes and learn lessons that you can use for the rest of your life. In business, it really is okay to come up short and not get the win you were seeking, something we often saw as we served in one of the big five banks as a foreclosure specialist. As a foreclosure specialists, we learned when we needed to start foreclosure, stop foreclosures, work with the trustees and the different liaisons at the bank. This type of inside knowledge and connections are invaluable in real estate.

Because I wrote the procedures for the foreclosure process, still currently used at that big five banks, it was easy for me to understand from the inside how to navigate through foreclosures. Learning this part of the real estate game is why it is important for us to help people on the outside. We saw and felt the grief foreclosure could bring upon a family. We took it personally and felt that we could really help; why not? Why not talk about foreclosure and how to navigate through foreclosure and the little moves you can make and help push back from a foreclosure or default. I was somebody on the inside who wrote the procedures for the foreclosure process, who now works outside to help the people prevent themselves from falling into foreclosure or how to navigate through foreclosure. You cannot beat that. One of our biggest things is we want to tell people what not to do because a lot of people will tell you what they think you need to do, but they will not tell you what not to do. We are going to help people know what not to do so you can really win. There are many things I hear that people do in real estate when they get into foreclosure or default that they really shouldn't do. You do not want to keep kicking the can down the road; you want to get resolved so you can move on.

We want to help people succeed, not just put temporary band-aids on things, but come up with solutions. In 2007, right before the market just completely went belly up, it was a whole lot of uncertainty. It was a lot of talk about what is going to happen next. What are we going to do? And sometimes, people panic! That is the last thing you want to do is panic in this game, do not panic. Too often, that is when bad decisions are made.

In the middle of panic that conjures up emotions, a knee jerk decision is made that way too often is regretted later on. Where you want and need to be is in a place where you understand all your options.

Also, I caution you from jumping from one thing to another because you heard it on a TV station or news channels. No! You want to be fully informed. So, in a situation or a climate, like right now(pandemic), people are either having their hours at work reduced, or maybe they are being laid off temporary. Naturally, one of the first things that kick in is how am I going to pay my bills? What is going to happen now, generally, especially when it comes to paying your mortgage, generally, some excitement starts to set in because it is like, what am I going to do now? One thing I learned from the real estate market crash in 2008, when there is temporary uncertainty in the market, banks will come up with different "help programs" that allow homeowners a chance to recover from the uncertainty in the market. You never know, maybe you cannot work for the next month because they shut everything down because of a pandemic and income has been reduced temporarily. Often the bank will offer what's called a Forbearance Program. A Forbearance Program provides the opportunity to get some relief, temporarily. Again, this is temporary, but it's something that can potentially give you some relief and help you bounce back. While the bank will offer you this forbearance option, please believe the bank will always want their money back. If you are going to have an income reduction for the foreseeable future, then the forbearance may not be something you want to do. However, if your reduction of income is temporary, a few months or even better, a couple of weeks or so, then the Forbearance Program would be worth consideration.

While working in the foreclosure department for one of the Big 5 banks, we would see people make a lot of permanent decisions based on something they are temporary going through. Decision making like this can carry on for years and people who stay in a reactive mindset instead of a proactive mindset end up eventually losing their house to foreclosure. Generally, our advice doesn't include temporary fixes. Still, forbearance programs in a climate like the pandemic or even an economic crash can help you keep your home from going into foreclosure or default until you can come up with a permanent solution. If you are approved for a forbearance program, you should then put your effort in getting that job back or a new job, get those hours back up, get that mortgage paid back up, and get back on your feet. The temporary pressure will reduce. So again, if you have any problems making your mortgage payments right now because of a temporary situation, your income is being reduced, then reach out to the bank and express interest in a forbearance program. The other side of that is if you're losing your job for the unforeseeable future or going to have an income reduction for the unforeseeable future, then a forbearance program may not be the right program for you.

In the case your income is reduced for the foreseeable future, then you should consider a loan modification; the bank may reduce payment, maybe even lower if you negotiate. If so, it won't be temporary and is basically a new loan, but keep in mind again, the bank wants their money. I saw it with my own two eyes while working at the bank; banks were reducing payments by a $100 or $75 with the max reduction of $200. Reducing your payments, $100, $200 is not really going to benefit you. While initially, it seems great that the bank reduced your payment, please believe that if you couldn't make your mortgage payment of $2000, having your payment reduced to $1900 will not help you but don't panic!

When panic sets in, desperation causes emotions to start flowing and people may just do anything. You remember when the pandemic first started, people panicked, went out and bought all the toilet paper, napkins, and water. Nothing was left in the stores! I'm not saying it's a bad decision to go buy those things, just helping you remember the panic that set in on so many people. Making decisions based on fear in real estate or dealing with your house is a big mistake. You want to make your decisions based on knowledge and understanding and knowing your options, not fear.

Chapter 2 (My Foreclosure Story)

This topic is going to be a little intimate. We're going to open up and give a little bit of our story on how we got to where we are today. I've had a few people contact me and ask, well, how did you become a foreclosure specialist? What took you to the path of real estate? How did you get there? My initial answer to the first question of how did you become a foreclosure specialist? I said that it was simply based upon getting all my houses foreclosed on when the market crashed. I mean, I learned a lot just by going through that. With that said, I remember in 2007 the market started getting funny. Now at this time, I'm in my twenties, I have amassed six properties. One of them, my primary domain, the rest of them I rented out. I rehabbed them all, so they were ready to be sold at top dollar whenever I was ready to put them on the market and I felt good about the potential, but one thing I was not doing, I was not paying attention and not tuned into where the market was headed. I'm just doing me, buying houses, fixing them up and renting them out. I'm thinking of being a millionaire here real soon, and not even paying attention to what is really happening in the economy. A lot of people were buying houses that they really couldn't afford, me included! During that time, real estate cost was so high that lenders were offering "interest-only" loans. Interest-only loan means that each time a monthly payment is made, you are only paying interest; NO principal is being paid off. What does that mean? You will never pay that house off; you will only pay interest year after year. Not only that those interest-only loans have an expiration date and once that loan expired, you would have to pay whatever the current interest rate was. During that time, the current interest rates were much higher than the "teaser", interest-only rate you had locked in for 3 or 5 years, so once your payment adjusted to the current market rate, your mortgage payments would jump upwards to $1000!! But all you heard back then was, "Oh, you are going to be good! You don't have to worry about it. Whenever it's time for that interest rate to adjust, you just sell the house. It will sell quick the market is hot! It doesn't even matter. You are going to be good".

That was not the case. When it was time for those interest rates to adjust, the market crashed and no one was buying houses at market value. Everything was sold at a deep discount which meant big losses! Always pay attention to what is going on in the market. What the market is doing, where it's going, and what's being forecasted. I wasn't thinking about any of that, I'm like buy, rehab, rent, and sale. That was the only thing I was thinking about. The market started getting more unstable and the next thing I know, the Crash of 2008. The banks stop lending money. Everything shut down. Everybody started losing their jobs. All my tenants lost their jobs. Every one of my tenants stopped paying rent very similar to what happened in 2020 with the pandemic. Kind of interesting how that fiasco repeated itself.

Plenty of times, I threw good money after bad, trying to win in a no-win situation. It didn't work. So, what did I have to do? I had to start liquidating, but of course, that was after throwing a bunch of good money after bad, trying to save the houses I talked about earlier. What ended up happening was I spent all my money trying to pay those mortgages each month and save a sinking ship but what ended up happening was I had no more money, but those monthly mortgages kept coming in. Therefore, I advise people to not throw good money after bad because it's not sustainable and all you do is end up broke and still having to start over. At least start over with all that good money in your pocket!

Now the scenario of starting over for me is that I'm working as a realtor in a market that crashed recently. Not only that, I had only been living in Los Angeles for about 4 years and I didn't know any local family member I could hit up or any colleagues or friends in a position to help. What I could do is start over from the bottom by creating a prospect list. Once I created that list, I had to start door knocking and cold calling. At that time, that plan wasn't going well. I had to begin thinking more critically and practical, I've only closed a few deals in the last couple of years and barely holding on right now. It was important for me to improve my income situation and while it was not a part of my plan, I started looking for additional employment. I came across a job opening at one of the big five banks. I thought I would apply to this and see what happens. It was in the foreclosure department, which was the exact place I needed to because foreclosure and real estate went hand in hand. This gave me an opportunity to get a behind the scenes look at how the bank does what it does. I just needed to load up my proverbial tool bag and apply what I learned to what I know and get ready to get back out here and perform in real estate with more knowledge and as you may have heard, "knowledge is power". So, lo and behold, I got the job. The only downside was it was in San Diego, which is not a downside to living in San Diego, so I moved from LA to San Diego.

I worked there for nearly three years, starting foreclosures, stopping foreclosures, working with the liaisons, and the trustees. Then I got an opportunity to write the procedures for the foreclosure process of a Big Five Bank. That was a big thing because I'm really a real estate person or investor guy at heart, but I'm on the other side writing the procedures for foreclosure processes. That was a real big deal, and I could hardly wait to get back in the real estate game. I understood how big that was and what that really meant for me going forward once I got back into real estate. It meant I was going to have a clear, concise idea of exactly how foreclosures work at the banks.

I contacted my friend and business partner because it was clear I am gaining a lot of game-winning information in this position, and it is possible for him to take the same steps. I ran the idea past him. He and his wife were already planning to return to California but to Los Angeles. I told him I'm working at one of the big five banks in the foreclosure department and the knowledge and ideas keep building. I said, "let's get this knowledge of the game and then take it back to LA in a couple years and win! So, he came, they moved to San Diego, he was hired at the bank. We were both working there, soaking up every bit of game we could get until one day it happened. They called a big meeting at the bank, had foreclosure, bankruptcy, the auto loan had everybody meet at once. Lost mitigation, everybody it's a building-wide meeting. And he said, "in order to normalize the workforce, we're going to have to shut the building down." Most people were devastated. I looked at my business partner and I said, it's time!

I came around the corner smiling while so many people were in tears. My business partner saw me, he said, "man, you need to relax. You're looking a little so happy right now." I told him "I am happy. You know what this means? Right now, it's time for us to get back to LA and get to it." And that's what we did we returned to Los Angeles and started focusing primarily on distressed sales. We were specialists working at the bank and this was where we started. We gained so much good game. You couldn't pay to get this information and training as well as insight and that was the idea of becoming foreclosure specialists. A little bit of on-the-job training and a lot of training at the bank in the foreclosure department, we say we're foreclosure specialists because we know what we were talking about. Real talk. We want to be able to give this game out to everybody and help you so you don't fall into foreclosure and get foreclosed on. However, if you do fall into foreclosure, we have the answers to get out and move on.

Chapter 3 (Forbearance Program)

During economic challenges in the real estate industry, there is a lot in the news and media about forbearance programs. Let's dig in a little deeper to really understand if using the forbearance program is really a good option for the situation; if you get behind on a mortgage payment, it's hard to get caught back up. It sounds elementary but believe me, some people will think the largest expenditure I have is the mortgage and if I use a little bit of my money allocated to the mortgage to pay the car note or maybe money for a road trip, I will replace it. I'm a hustler and I'll make the money. The next month, I did not have enough to make up the difference and now I am behind on my mortgage. They didn't make more money. They couldn't afford to catch back up. This is how default starts to happen.

So, you hear about a forbearance program. A forbearance program is when the bank allows you to pause or reduce your mortgage payments for a limited period. For example, if you qualify for the forbearance program, the bank can allow you to not make payments on your mortgage for up to 6 months and then the missed payments will be tacked onto the backend of your mortgage. Or the bank can reduce your payment for 6 months and then tack on the money from those reduced payments to the backend of your mortgage. You must be careful with forbearance programs because some banks will require all the missed payments to be paid in full once the forbearance is over instead of tacking it on to the back of your loan. To determine if the forbearance program is a good fit for your situation, first and foremost think, this house is your primary residence. Forbearance programs come with risks, so taking risks with the place that you lay your head should be highly scrutinized and thought out.

There are many people who have money saved up and can make 3 or more payments for emergency purposes if needed. If you have significant savings and can make your mortgage payment, then do it. Once you get behind on your mortgage payments, it's hard to catch back up. Some people think they can just do a forbearance as a way to stack some extra money up, but it remains a common theme, I thought that I could catch up if I missed just one or two payments, but that didn't happen. You did not have the savings to catch up on those forbearance payments, but it sounded like a good idea at the time. I can stack a little more money, but you still got to pay it back. What people didn't realize is that some banks want a lump sum payment once the forbearance is over. It happens like this, you get in a forbearance program, and you don't pay three months of your mortgage payments, then that fourth month, the bank indicates the need for a lump sum payment of those previous three months and the fourth month as they are all due. That's detrimental and a pending disaster if you did not have the 3 months saved up. When you stop making mortgage payments on your house, you just don't want the downward spiral to begin, and you cannot get caught up. Something else happens the next month. Then something else happens the following month. And you just can't seem to get caught back up. So why risk it?

Then, there are some who think about it this way. 'Oh, well, the bank will put my missed payments on the back end of my loan. And I'll just pay it over the course of the next 30 years of my loan!' Well, did you hear what you just said? You are going to pay interest on that amount that you missed in mortgage payments over the course of the next 30 years, along with paying it off on that 30th year? That's crazy thinking, that's a wreck looking for a time to happen. Yeah. Initially, you don't feel it, so you postpone it thinking you will just add it on the back end. We work to win in the real estate game. We don't want to do things we don't have to do. We don't need to add on to the mortgage. If you don't have to, don't do it.

Don't play with the fire. But some people need the forbearance program, especially if they are not working, don't have regular income and don't have any savings. So immediately, they must pause those payments. Now most likely there's a bigger underlying issue there, you may be living above your means. If, after one month of not working, you are unable to make your mortgage payment. That means you don't make enough money for bills that you have. If everything has to go right each month for you to pay all your bills, then you are living above your means. You should be able to go at least three months without making money and still be able to make your payments comfortably. If you can't do it that means you are not living within your means. If you are one of those people who, after a month or two of not working and you immediately can't pay your mortgage. You need to really think about your financial situation and really analyze some things.

The idea is to analyze your bills to see what you need cut to bring your bills down. Sit back and think about all the things that you spend each month. Put it all on paper at the top of the list should be utilities, food, mortgage, transportation, and communication. These are the necessities; first and foremost, if you don't have enough money for these line items here, then the tough reality is you can no longer afford that home. If the biggest bill that you're having a problem with is your mortgage payment, you're living above your means. There's an old saying men lie, women lie, numbers don't. The Numbers are going to tell the truth. What do you do if you are living above your means? I'm going to say, humble yourself because you should probably sell your house. I suspect you didn't want to hear that, but that's a fact if you can't afford it. No sense in trying to put all that pressure on yourself month after month after month; you might as well go ahead and sell. Remember you want to win and there may be value in selling the house to get you ready to buy your next one. This time you will be wiser and smarter. That's what it's all about. Don't have somebody charge you a fee to tell you what you want to hear and then you still end up in foreclosure. I've seen it time and time again, unfortunately; when times of uncertainty come around, it's all type of finesse plays that people come up with just to get little money grabs out of you. Do not fall for any third parties telling you what you want to hear. It's a numbers game and if the numbers don't add up and it doesn't make sense for you to keep the house, you know what you need to do and don't have anybody tell you what you want to hear.

Start over. It's okay to start over. It's okay to sell and take a do-over. You get caught up in this is my house attitude, but it is also a means to get a new house. With that attitude, you start making bad decisions to try to keep your house.

Overall, the main point to get across is to think twice before deciding to go into a forbearance program because down the road, you must make that lump sum payment. Some might just be okay with the bank, tacking those payments on the back end. But for those of you who have savings, don't do it. Don't get behind because anything could start happening once you get behind and you don't want to play with fire on your primary residence. If you're really, really in a position where you cannot make those mortgage payments, then definitely talk to the bank about reducing payments or partial payments for a while or even the forbearance program, but please understand the consequences of getting behind on that mortgage.

Chapter 4 (Loan Modification)

Let's jump right to it and get into hardships. What do you do when you start experiencing hardship? Naturally, hardship can come in various ways or different forms. You could have income reduction, you could have increased house expenses, a divorce, maybe a death of one of the borrowers or some sort of disaster, or maybe you had a business failure. Either way, all these things reduce your income, in some form or fashion. You can no longer make your payments on your mortgage, and you need to know what to do next. Reach out to the bank and ask about the various workout programs they have to help you. Most banks implement different hardship programs for borrowers to be able to apply for and most of the hardship programs revolve around forbearance programs, which we spoke about in the previous chapter or loan modifications.

Let's just take a step back and check out where the loan modification or the so-called loan modification comes from. It's coming from the lender. The lender is a bank. The bank is in the business of lending out money and charging interest or making money. So normally when you own your home and you're looking to make changes to the mortgage that you have, you call your loan officer up and say, I'm looking into refinancing my mortgage. I want to do a refinance. Now let's examine the steps for a loan modification. You have been in default on your mortgage for a minimum of 3 months and you decide that you want to work it out with the bank to try and remain in the house.

That is when you reach out to the loss mitigation department and ask if we can work something out? I want to try to stay in my home. And they agree to work out a loan modification. So, they take an application, take all the supporting income documentation, and send it to underwriters to make a decision. Remember, they are in the business of making money.

When you do a refinance (refi), you can refinance because you are current on your mortgage. However, if you are doing a loan modification, it's because you are in default on your mortgage. The only thing that is different about these two scenarios is the fact that you were current on your mortgage in one and late on your mortgage in the other scenario. As far as the bank, the process was the same. Albeit a different department, they took an application, they still got income documentation to support that application and sent it to underwriters like a normal loan. So, what I'm trying to tell you is a loan modification is a refinance. You're applying for a new loan with the bank. So, you still need to qualify for the loan modification, which means you still must show income. Let's just say you are trying to do a loan modification on a half-million-dollar mortgage. You may have been making $100,000 a year when you first bought the house. So, of course, you were able to qualify for that loan. But now that you're in default and the main reason you are into default is because you had a reduction in income. So now your income is $50,000. Do you really expect to still qualify for a half a million-dollar loan? So be real with yourself. When discussing loan modifications, it does not mean that the bank is going to reduce your payments to what you're making now. Unfortunately, some develop a false sense that the bank is going to help. Remember that the bank is in the money-making business. And they're going to do what makes them money. You are making $30,000 less a year than when you first qualified for the mortgage doesn't make sense for the bank to give you a loan modification. The bank looks at it like this file is heading to foreclosure; they can no longer afford this house. So, people must really understand loan modifications are nothing more than a refinance for people who are in default. You still must qualify for the loan! To qualify, you must show good income! You make 30k less a year than when you first bought the home. That means you don't qualify, or it will be hard for you to qualify because you don't show the income needed to qualify for a 500k mortgage as of now.

Just so we are clear a loan modification is when the bank rewrites the loan that you originally had, reduce your payments, making it a new loan and they are making money. This is the typical workout program that customers often tries to qualify for. Now, the question is, are you getting this loan modification with the intention of keeping the house and being able to start making those payments? Or are you getting this loan modification knowing that you still can't afford the mortgage and in a couple of months, you're going to end up in a re-default. You must really understand why you're getting that loan modification. Let's just say the bank only reduce your payments $75. That's not going to really help you to be able to afford that monthly payment. It gives you that false sense of the "the bank is working with me." However, deep down, you know that you still can't afford it. When you get a loan modification at the bank, most people think that they drop your payments three, four, or $500. You think, Oh yeah, I'm going to have this low payment and it's going to be much more affordable.

Please understand this again; the bank always wants their money! So, to think that they're just going to reduce your payments $500 is not likely. Stay in the real world here. You don't want to start dreaming and making up things in your mind that can happen because somebody told you what they heard or what they saw on TV. For instance, someone may tell you they got the bank to forgive all their back pay owed from missing payments. However, what they really got was a silent second loan on their house to cover the back pay owed. A silent second is a mortgage placed on your home in addition to your first mortgage. Usually, you don't have to make monthly payments on the silent second however, when it's time to sell or refinance your home, that silent second must be paid off with interest included. For example, the bank gave you a $20,000 silence second to cover the back payments owed, but you're really paying them back because they just added another lien on your property. Most people who get silent seconds don't understand it's still a loan; all they know is the bank "forgave" their back payments and their payment was reduced. Don't believe what people say because a lot of the time, you are getting half of the true story. We want to tell you all the story and give you that real talk so you can make an educated decision. The question you want to ask yourself is If you are attempting to get a loan modification, does it make sense to go forward with that loan modification if you are getting a silent second to cover the backpay or getting a minimal payment reduction?

If they only reduce your payments $75, but your income has been reduced by maybe $600 a month. You still really can't afford the mortgage with only a $75 payment reduction. So, some real tough decisions must start being made. You must start really looking at things as really like a business decision now because you got to do what's best for you and your family. Now you got to understand that a lot of times a loan modification is not the best thing for you. The best thing for you to do is to remove yourself from that debt, start all over and then go buy something else in your price range that you can afford. Yeah, a lot of people don't like to hear that, but always remember, don't throw good money after bad and starting over is ok.

Often, homeowners say, "you are a real estate broker, and you just want to sell my house." Not really. I'm trying to tell you; you need to sell your house because eventually, that's what's going to end up happening. You either must sell your house or the bank will foreclose on your house. So why keep making these payments throwing good money after bad for, to end up still being foreclosed on or still having to sell. You could have kept all that money and sold it earlier, moved on to the next situation, and then be ready to get back in the buying market. People got to really think about this. You got to really think about the best options for you. And sometimes you are getting shortsighted being stuck in what's happening now, but you must look down the road and see the light at the end of tunnel. Next thing you know 2 years down the road, you are buying another home.

The best result is keeping that $15,000 or $20,000 in your pocket that you were going to end up spending on a bad loan modification. Many times, what people fail to understand is that loan modification only reduces payments a small amount. The bank is anticipating you going back into foreclosure. When I worked at the bank, going through thousands of foreclosure responses, reading people's letters that they send to the bank about not having AC in the summer and no heat in the winter, doing everything they can to save money to try and make this mortgage payment. Oh, can you please reduce my payments? From inside the bank, no matter what the letter said, you send them what amounts to standard procedure reply aka Canned Comment. It doesn't matter what is said, no matter how you play it or word it, the job dictated was to read the letter and then send them these canned comments and that's that.

It's like, yeah, we'll give you a loan modification and if you can manage to keep paying, then that's good for you. If not, you'll be back in foreclosure. The bank may choose to give you another chance at a loan modification. I've seen people get two, three, or four loan modifications and now they are on the fifth modification, they've defaulted on all of them and they're still sending letters asking for another loan modification. The bank deals with this because they look at the bigger picture and already wrote off this debt as bad debt. So, any money that they can get is just extra money; whether they sell it through a foreclosure sale, short sell or REO, it's extra money for the bank. Keep this in mind, if you are in foreclosure or default, the bank will write off your loan as bad debt; therefore any extra money they can get out of you through a loan modification is extra money for the bank. It's not set up for you to succeed it's set up for the bank to make money because that is what they do!

Chapter 5 (Don't Throw Good Money After Bad)

Well, you have gotten a notice of default assigned on your property and there are a few what not to do when facing perhaps one of the more shattering things loaded on your plate. This is a well-traveled road heading in the direction of foreclosure. Often people always work to inform you as to what to do. It's like, you should do this, and you need to do that, but much of the information you are being given is bad advice.

The best advice anyone should give is don't throw good money after bad money. It bears repeating again, do not throw good money after bad money. That is the key to keeping your liquidity, holding onto adequate "cash in your pocket". When things are starting to go array, it's not always the best idea to shell out your cash to try to save a losing situation, it's not going to save it. You're still going to crash as you could be facing foreclosure. The bank loan modification has helped, but you still haven't been able to make your payments because of a substantial reduction of income. Regardless of how you got on this road, you've had a major reduction in income; you have this loan modification, the bank has reduced your payments by $75. Now you know, reducing your payments by $75 is not helping you as the road narrows. That doesn't put you in a better position to say, "Oh, I can, I can make my payments". You postponed the obvious and it didn't help you out. You know that you still don't make enough to make this monthly payment.

Do not continue to make these payments scrounging up your last nickels, dimes, and quarters. Going out thinking I can sell this and sell that to get the money for the mortgage this month. Don't keep doing that because you can't sustain it, and it just won't work. To help drive the point home to you, now that you have sold your stuff, your car breaks down. You are looking at a $700 repair bill and you know you must have a car to get around. That's how you handle your business or go to work every day. You spend the $700 from the stuff you sold, and you cannot make that mortgage payment again. So, you're back in the same position, throwing good money after bad. Once you get behind, it is rare to get caught back up unless you get a lump sum of cash or a new job that pays well.

Most times, people get behind, throwing good money after bad trying to save the situation, but the inevitable still happens. In 2007, when the market was crashing, I hit a point where all my tenants lost their jobs, all of them! Back then, I had five rental properties; I rehabbed them and then rented them out for a while with the intent of selling them within 6 months. I thought I was ready. The houses were fixed up everything's nice tenants were paying rent on time. And then suddenly, the crash begins. People start losing their jobs and naturally when they lose their job, they can't pay their rent. I have five rental properties and five additional mortgages along with my mortgage for my primary home. Now I knew I could not sustain paying six different mortgages, one being my primary house mortgage. I knew I couldn't sustain that for a long period of time but because I wanted to believe that things were going to get better. I said, hey, I'm going to do everything I can to save these or hold onto these properties. I don't want to mess my credit up. I want to keep it good. You know, that's one of the issues on this road that we face once things start going bad. We have always been taught to keep our credit good. Oh, I don't want to mess my credit up. I've got to pay these mortgages. I got to do this. I must do this. So, I did everything I could to pay those mortgages every month, which I knew I couldn't sustain. I knew I couldn't keep doing it. Kept doing it, kept doing it until what? Now, I have no more money. And guess what? The mortgage payments are still due. I spent all that good money I had trying to save a bad situation and I still ended up in that bad situation, throwing good money after bad. We don't want to do that.

The next thing we don't do is sit and sulk. Another term I often use is living in Candyland. Man! It's easy to do that. I'm getting ready to lose my house. Oh man, this is my baby. My house is my domain, my castle; I'm sick. It's easy to do that. I did that a little bit myself. I was like, oh, I'm getting ready to lose all my properties, man. Why, why is this happening? Why, oh man, what can I do to save them all of this and that. And then one day, I snapped right out of it. I was like, wait a minute. I'm sitting here sulking. There is nothing changing. Do not live in Candyland. We're in the real world out here. You can't sit in Candyland and hope and wish that things will get better. Oh, I hope that the bank one day just understands my pain and what I'm going through and just writes down my mortgage. Oh, I wish that I'll get a bunch of money and I could just pay my mortgage current, I need to buy lottery tickets, or the bank will do something for me; they talk about helping and being a friend in commercials. These are all statements of somebody who's living in Candy land.

Wake up; we are in the real world out here; you cannot sit in Candyland thinking about what somebody should do for you. The first thing I need to do to get out of this hole is to stop digging deeper and to change the road I am traveling. We have been reactionary and responding to what was coming next instead, we must be proactive. We got to do what's necessary to get back on our feet.

Lastly, do not expect the bank to help you out. They are not required to help you out, but they can give you a chance if you qualify for a loan modification or a forbearance program. From working in the bank in the foreclosure department, I already knew the bank was giving a chance to people who still didn't have a chance because you must qualify and most people who are in foreclosure or headed towards foreclosure, they can't qualify for that current loan that they're in now because they don't make as much money as they were making when they initially got that loan. So, the bank will ask to submit your financials, as well as this and that. Getting a loan modification is like a whole new pre-approval process again for a loan. Which means the bank will look at your income and be like, oh, your income reduced. And of course, you are like, yeah of course my income has been reduced that's why I'm behind. In the foreclosure dept, I saw time and time again that if you were lucky to get a loan modification, the bank usually would reduce the payments a maximum of $200 on average. Some people would get more of a reduction, but that was not normal. Keep this in mind the bank is about making that money. You must keep that in perspective and understand that you got to do what's best for you and your family. A lot of times, a loan modification may not be your best option because you are just kicking the can down the road. Most times, the best option is the one you don't want to do, which is to sell the home, start saving money again and start over. Starting over is not a bad thing, especially since you start from a place of more insight and knowledge of the real estate game.

Chapter 6 (It's Not Your Fault But It Is Your Responsibility)

My business partner Walter coined the phrase, "It's not your fault, but it is your responsibility" let me repeat that, "It's not your fault, but it is your responsibility". We all know the times that we're in right now with this pandemic; it had nothing to do with us per se.

I mean it's not any one person's fault that this happened, but it happened. With that said it's our responsibility to figure out how to navigate through this. We can't just sit back and do nothing. Check this out. Everyone has been late to work because you've been stuck in traffic due to a car accident. Or if you live in LA on that 110 freeway, it could be as simple as a couch in the middle of the freeway, taking up one and a half lanes and having everything backed up. People jumping from lane to lane, trying not to hit the couch, got traffic backed up. Now it's not your fault that there was an accident on the freeway, or it's not your fault that somebody dropped the couch off the bed of their truck and left it on the freeway and now everybody's, jumping around lane to lane, causing traffic backup. None of that's your fault. However, it doesn't change the fact that you were late for your own meeting and presentation at work. Still got to take responsibility, right? Don't nobody want to hear traffic was backed up or something was in the middle of the road? No, "ain't" nobody trying to hear that. So, you got to take responsibility. Similarly, many homeowners and small business owners are facing a daunting challenge during uncertain times; circumstances far beyond our control have threatened people's livelihoods. What's a small business to do when they just opened a couple months ago, and now they're being told they got to shut it down due to pandemic? You have no control over that. The only thing you can control is how to navigate around it. How to figure out how to keep generating some income, same thing with a homeowner you've been told you can't go to work, stay at home. You were laid off temporarily and have no money coming in, it's not so fault, but it is your responsibility to be well informed of your options. And that's the key, being well informed. As a homeowner, you got to know, okay, it's not my fault that they told us, we had stayed home and I got relieved of my job, but it's definitely my responsibility to make sure that I'm able to keep my house. And if I can't keep my house, I need to know what the next steps are. It's your responsibility.

Often, when things happen beyond your control, some people tend to just sit back and be reactive and just react to everything that's thrown at them. And just try to figure it out versus being proactive. Those that are proactive come out in a better situation. So, in life, when things beyond your control happen, that may not be your fault, but it is absolutely your responsibility to maneuver in the right way so that it doesn't affect you as much as it can. Keep pushing everybody, stay strong; you are going to make it through.

Chapter 7 (Best Choice)

We really like to give up the game so that all people can experience the American Dream of homeownership. Giving up the game will really help people win in real estate and make the right choices. I can tell you I experienced the scenario of foreclosure. I sat and did nothing, then felt the weight of the world on my shoulders that kept me being disgusted and depressed. It's not a good place to be. I recall during the recession in 2008, I came to the realization I was going to have to sell all my properties. Now I was okay with selling the investment properties, the rentals and all of that. I didn't have a problem with that, but my condo was the first property I ever bought! I did not want to let that go and was deep into the drama; this is my first piece of property. I can't let this go. I'm going to have to do whatever it takes to keep this, my baby. I can't let, I can't let it go. They aren't going to just take it from me. Over the course of the next year and a half of doing loan modifications, then getting denied. You get another opportunity for a loan modification. Of course, denied I'm an entrepreneur, meaning I could not show much money on paper. So constantly being denied. On a day of what must have been divine intervention, it hits me to get out of this mess, and this drama-filled mess.

I need to make better decisions to move forward with my life. And it was one of the best decisions I ever made. It was then that I chose to remove the weight of the world from my shoulders by selling my baby, my first piece of property. So, I understand the feelings and emotions. And the terrible decisions made while in that state of mind. I could have benefited from this book and somebody giving me the game in a way that I could manage it. I took emotions out and used logic and knowledge to make the right choice, not the emotions that kept me from taking the right step.

When I decided to move on from foreclosure, other elements of my life I never knew were being affected began to free up. I didn't even realize I was being shackled because I have been knee-deep in the emotions of bouncing from one emotional emergency to the next it's like your life is being caught up in a pinball machine. I stopped answering the door. I stopped checking my mail and I really wouldn't answer the phone because I thought it was either bill collectors or somebody talking about how they could help me out with my situation. And, in doing that, I'm missing opportunities. Not everybody knocking on my door was a bill collector; not everyone calling was a bill collector or trying to "help" me out of my situation. So, I end up missing out on some important things. But I was out of the game and did not want to play, let alone not win. Not win? What? I did not want to lose, so I needed to do something and stop dodging the reality.

You know, it wasn't so bad, I had been running from this reality, but it wasn't that bad once I stopped running. And that's what I really realize that starting over is not that bad at the end of the day because you can buy another house or houses! I then took a few steps to get back on track to buying another home after this foreclosure experience.

I finally decided to sell my first piece of property, although it hurt me, and I felt like I failed and all the emotions that came with it. Once I made the conscious decision to sell it, move on and start over. I could breathe a lot easier, and the weight fell off my shoulders. I had a plan and I realized other opportunities were coming my way because I changed my mindset; I could see the opportunities coming again. I decided to sell that property, move on from the foreclosure drama, and discovered that the bank gives relocation funds. Already getting started off on better footing with the extra money. I can get up, and I can get back into the gym and research my next step with greater energy; it became much easier. I'm making conscious decisions to get out of a bad situation. And by doing that, I'm creating good situations, new opportunities, and other positive things in my life. That's the mindset you need, positive affirmations about moving forward, feeling motivated and rejuvenated all because I decided to move on. I am taking my life back. While not even realizing it, I had been stuck in the paradigm that I'm about to lose my house, my property. But after I got to that point where I had no other smart choices, I moved on.

Chapter 8 (The Bounce Back)

After you have either sold your home or it was foreclosed on, you have to figure out how to bounce back. I ended up getting 2 houses foreclosed on and then short-selling the remaining properties at a major loss. I still ended up having a mountain of debt from all the costs I incurred rehabbing the homes. My debt was in the hundreds of thousands and the best option for me was to file Chapter 7 Bankruptcy. I was humiliated when I finally came to that conclusion. Here I was supposed to be a millionaire by 30 and instead, I'm filing BK and starting completely over with minimal money in my pocket. The Bankruptcy just absolutely killed my credit score and for about 2 years, I couldn't even get approved from any credit cards.

For me to bounce back and put myself back into a position to purchase another home, I first needed to repair my credit. When going through a foreclosure your credit will be damaged because you have been late on a mortgage for multiple months, then you add bankruptcy to the situation and it just kills your credit score. I had to build my credit back up by getting positive trade-lines on my credit report. Finally after a few years, I got approved for a credit card of $500. Once I got the card, I would be charged $100 on it, then pay it ALL off once the bill was due. I did this for 6 months and I saw the credit score change in a good way. Now, because I had one positive trade line on my credit report, I could get another credit card to have a 2nd positive trade line. So, I kept doing this same process for the next 2 years on both credit cards. Taking these little steps were important and I had to remain patient because I was coming back, bigger and better than ever! Two positive trade-lines on your credit is all you need to build that score back up. Bankruptcy is the last option, so if you have collections on your credit report, reach out to all the collection agencies on your credit report and settle with them. I realized that it was better to have the money at the time you are trying to settle each account that way, you can pay in full and you can negotiate a deep discount because you are ready to settle right then.

While I was building my credit back up, I built my reserve funds back up too. I started saving money, all additional income really helped to save money and I knew my savings account was looking better. I kept all my expenses low and made various sacrifices, whether it was no cable or no gym membership. Sometimes I felt tempted to rock & roll and impulse buy some stuff that I didn't really need every time I made some extra money, but I remembered the down payment and closing cost and that motivated me to just keep stacking it up. Even though I had a public record on my credit report (BK), I could still get my credit back up to par by the method I explained a few paragraphs ago. After nearly two years of working on improving that credit score and saving money, I reached out to a loan officer to get pre-approved again and bang! It was on; taking those steps to rebuild my financial future was the smartest move I could make. I was back in the win column, smarter and wiser! That's what it's like to lift that weight off your shoulders, all that stuff that I was going through, all that stuff that I was dealing with, all of those emotions, all of that drama did not even matter anymore, you've moved on and that is a great feeling. Everything in this book I have been through, so trust me when I say all you have to do is keep focused, develop your goals and take one step at a time and most of all, look for solutions, not temporary band-aids.

Chapter 9(The Process)

Now that you have bounced back fully, got your credit score back up and got your saving back up, it's time to get back into the buying market! There are many things I want you to be prepared for the next go around when making, perhaps, the largest purchase you make in your life. Purchasing a home is generally the largest purchase people make, so you have to be prepared for large and small things and work to eliminate any surprises. That way, when you sit down to sign papers, you do so from a position of knowledge and not just simply hearing the talk but not able to process it all because you did not know!

Obviously, being prepared financially is the first step; it starts with your credit and credit score, referred to as FICO score. The credit score is the numerical representation of your credit worthiness, which is maintained at the major credit bureaus, Experian, Equifax, Transunion. Generally, you need a FICO around a 620 to get pre-approved for a home loan. Sometimes, there are programs out there where a score as low as 580 can work and the better programs start at 670. With a score of 620, there are plenty of lenders that can get you a home loan.

Check your credit at each of the 3 credit bureaus Experian, Equifax, and TransUnion. There you will see the history of your collection, any late credit payments, bankruptcies, and judgements, all of which can affect your credit. The banks will look at your credit history to determine whether they will pre-approve you for a home loan or not. So, if you have collections, you need to settle and get those paid off. Most times, the bank requires you to pay these collections off before the loan application can get you approved. Therefore, call them and work out a plan to settle. Generally, you can settle 50 60% on what you initially owed. If you have the money right then and you're ready to pay for it that day, do it! That is why you keep stacking your money up when you are coming back. Forget the road trip, the concert, and the partying because I will be back winning in a couple of years!

Next, look over your credit report and see if you have any recent late payments. Current late payments on your credit report will be problematic for the bank; make sure you get caught up on all your current debts. There are some banks out there that will still approve you for a mortgage with late payments showing on your credit report; however you may have to pay more points (fees for obtaining the loan) and you may have a higher than usual interest rate. The goal is to get the best interest rate for the least number of points.

We are talking about what you need to do to be prepared to get a good loan with the best interest rate possible. Get a handle on your finances, make sure that you have enough reserves in the bank for down payment, closing costs, and additional reserves. You got to figure out how much you want to put down to purchase your home. Do you want to put 3.5% down and get an FHA loan? FHA doesn't lend you money for a mortgage; instead, you get a loan from an FHA approved lender like a bank or another financial institution. FHA loans are Federally insured loans which means if you were to default on that loan, the government will ensure the bank is paid back, they are making money. This reduces the lender risk on the loan and makes it easier for a borrower to qualify. Or do you want to go conventional and 5%-20% down? A conventional loan typically has stricter credit requirements than FHA loans because the government doesn't insure conventional loans. Keep in mind that if you put less than 20% down, you will also have to pay monthly PMI along with your mortgage. PMI is private mortgage insurance which also ensures the lender in case you default on the loan. Usually, people who go conventional (put more money down) are looked at as more financially sound because they put more money down and have a higher credit score.

For example, let's say you want to purchase a home for $300k. If you were to go FHA, then you would have to put $10,500 (3.5%) down plus closing costs. Your monthly payments, principal and interest is a mortgage payment of $1901(3.25% interest rate); Monthly Taxes, $312 (in California taxes are roughly 1.25% of purchase price); Monthly Insurance, $62 (insurance is roughly .25% of purchase price); PMI, $250(PMI is roughly 1% of purchase price); Total Monthly payment for FHA loan of 300k is $2,525.

Let's say you want to go conventional and put 20% (60k down payment) down your monthly payments would include: Principal and Interest mortgage payment of $1437 (3.185 interest rate. Of course, you get a better rate when you put more money down); Monthly Taxes, $312; Monthly Insurance, $62; No PMI because 20% was put down; Total Monthly payment for conventional loan with 20% down is $1811.

Next you need to show proof that there are some reserves in the bank after making payments. Yes, after spending all that money, the bank's going to want to see that you got reserves still, so three to six months; of course, six months reserve is the best way to go. Banks love seeing additional reserves, and it bodes well on your approval process.

So, make sure you have enough money in the bank to jump in and buy a house because it's not something that you can buy with minimal money in the bank. Many people try to buy houses with minimal money down and minimal savings, but that's not the recipe for success. Most people who take that route are highly likely to go under and eventually lose their homes to foreclosure. So, we're talking about succeeding in the real estate game. We want to show you how to win and to win, you must prepare, stack and save that money! Here is another gem: do not make any large purchases once you get pre-approved for a home loan. Let me repeat that. Do not make any large purchases, it sounds elementary, but believe it or not, I've had clients do just that. We were getting ready loan documents in a couple of days and her birthday comes and she's like, yeah. You know what I did for my birthday, I bought myself a diamond ring! You did what?

I bought myself a diamond ring. I deserve it. Don't worry. Don't worry. It's cool. I paid cash. I said so the bank is going to see that you just made this large purchase right before you're going to make the largest purchase in your life. Well, they passed on her and it fell out of escrow. No large purchases after you get pre-approval, no large purchases before you get pre-approved. You're trying to get pre-approved and need to show as minimal debt as possible.

After putting your finances in order, the next step would be to go to a lender seeking a pre-approval letter. Be prepared for the banks to ask you to provide previous month's bank statements, the last two years of tax returns, W2's, a copy of your driver's license, and social security card. And now you wait on the lender to come back and let you know what amount you are pre-approved for, then you can start shopping. Too many times, people jump the gun and start shopping before being pre-approved. Once you get pre-approved, you know what you can afford to buy. A lot of times It is reality check as to what you want versus what you can afford. It's important that you stay within your mean, whether you are a first-time homebuyer, a move-up buyer, or a buyer coming back into the game from foreclosure.

I had one client tell me before they were pre-approved for a home that they wanted to live in Culver City only. I'm like, Ooh, Culver City area, how much you make a year? I was like, you're not going to be able to live in Culver City making that. It's expensive out there; think about this, slow is fast and fast is slow. Trying to do things too fast often means you waste time having to go back to correct your mistakes when if you had just slowed down and did things right the first, it would have taken the same amount of time as having to rush through something than go back to correct the mistakes. Start with a nice starter home in your price range. Make sure you do things to the house to increase the value. Hopefully, when it's time to sell the starter home, you will be making more money and you will have a lot of equity that you can use as a down payment to eventually get that home in Culver City!

Back to your pre-approval. Now you have pre-approval, and you know what price points you can afford based on the previous calculation. You are ready to shop for a home of your own. Perhaps you know a realtor and one has been referred to you after great recommendations. The realtor will pull houses from the Multiple Listing Service (MLS) and start sending you all the latest houses for sale. You want to look it over for those you would like to visit. A hint I always give my clients is before we look at the inside, you may need to drive over and check the neighborhood out. If you're not familiar with that area, drive over there at night as well. Make sure it is a place you want to live. As a young real estate agent, I would drive my clients around going to the place they had selected. And as soon as we turn on the street, they're like, "Nope, next one!".

We drove all the way out here and immediately after turning onto the street, and you don't like it. So, I had to start letting my clients know it is important for them to get invested in the selection process. You're going to make the biggest purchase of your life, so get more invested by driving to make sure you like the area. When the Real Estate Agent drives you around, there is an expectation that you will stop and go inside the house. At your own leisure, go check it out and save yourself and your agent some time and even anxiety. You schedule the time with the realtor, and you visit houses with the potential of becoming your home. If you find one, you like it, then put an offer wait and see if it gets accepted or not. In Los Angeles, it is customary that you're going to have to put in multiple offers on different properties before you get your first house. There is a lot of competition for home right now. Be prepared for that and understand that that is competition. In areas not so competitive, you may get your offer accepted immediately. Also, you may not get the first house that you like. Don't take it personal; keep looking. When you get an offer accepted, send the deposit to escrow, escrow is opened and now it's time to get the party started. After escrow is opened typically, you're going to get several disclosures, it's going to be a lot of paperwork; do your best to read through it, take notes and ask questions. You want to make sure that you read over that stuff and be fully informed on the type of house that you're buying and the condition of that house you want. I mean, it's the largest purchase that you're going to typically make in your life. You want to know what you are getting, so be informed, read everything, and ask questions, do not be afraid to ask questions. Some people are intimidated by asking questions because they think it might be a dumb question. Nothing's a dumb question. You are doing something you have never done before; it ok to not know everything. Get it out of your mind; no question is dumb. And even if you have bought a house before things change, no questions are dumb.

So always ask questions and get the inspections. Inspections are critical as you want a home inspection to include electrical, plumbing, foundation, roof, water heater, termite inspection and even sewer inspection. The inspector will charge a fee that is well worth the expense, especially on older homes. The inspector fee is normally based on the square footage of the home; for example, a 2000 sq ft home is around $400-$500 for inspection. The inspector will tell you everything wrong with the house, so you'll be informed and knowing what you are buying, and it helps you negotiate price of the home or improvements you want made before purchase. Don't fret, there's always going to be some issue with every house; it seems almost just customary. You can waive inspections, but this is one of the biggest deals of your life, it's highly recommended so you do this deal from a perspective of knowledge of the house and strength of the pre-approval letter.

Typically, the bank, your lender, will order an appraisal which is included in the cost of the home, and you will pay for it. This will inform you as to the value of the house. Their appraisal is going to come in around what you offered on the house, but there are times when the appraisal comes in less. And when that happens, you go back and renegotiate and say, 'Hey, you know this house is appraised for less than what my offer, so I want you to bring the cost down.' Sometimes the seller will bring it down, but then there are others who will say, 'Nah, that is what you offered, that's what you would pay, so you need to pay that', and are now just stuck on that price. Big decision time now, is this a deal-breaker? Always be able to walk away from a deal but if your heart is set, then you will need to pay the additional in the form of your down payment. Get that appraisal.

Then comes the loan documents. The banks will be sending you a whole bunch of paperwork. It will look overwhelming because it's a lot. But this is a big deal, your house, your kingdom, your domain, and you will need to sign that stuff. When I bought my first few houses, I would read every document. They gave me all those loan documents, and whether I understood it or not was another thing, but I would read it. There's a lot of stuff there, but make sure you know what type of loan you're getting. Just work to be fully informed; that is a major part of purchasing a home, be fully informed. Today, with the ability to Goggle for information, being fully informed is easier but also, write down your questions and ask them when you sit down to sign.

Once all loan docs are signed you will need to wire you portion of the downpayment and closings, then the bank funds the rest of the loan. Now the deal is funded. So next thing up is recording the deed in your name and after that, you are the Homeowner! Buying a home can be stressful, but here is the reward! Your castle! Many things will occur during this journey they come you resolve it on to the next until the end. There will be little things and nuances and curveballs that get thrown in. But all in all, once you make that purchase and you get those keys, you know, made a great purchase. After living in your home for a few years, getting accustomed to the increased expenses of homeownership, and saving some more money, you will be ready to purchase that first rental property! Stay tuned for guidance on when is the right time to purchase the first rental! Coming Soon.

Don't miss out!

Visit the website below and you can sign up to receive emails whenever Emmitt Hayes publishes a new book. There's no charge and no obligation.

https://books2read.com/r/B-A-NYVS-KGYWB

BOOKS 2 READ

Connecting independent readers to independent writers.

Also by Emmitt Hayes

Giving up the Game: How to Win in Real Estate

About the Author

Prior to starting his own realty and investment Company(Hayes Realty ,founded 2014), Emmitt was employed at JP Morgan Chase as Operation Specialist in the foreclosure Department. During his tenure with Chase, Emmitt authored the procedures for the Departmental Foreclosure processes. In 2002, Emmitt graduated from Park University located in Parkville, MO with a Bachelor of Arts degree in Business Finance.

www.ingramcontent.com/pod-product-compliance
Lightning Source LLC
Chambersburg PA
CBHW050615160726
48003CB00003B/1191